WIFE
OF
LIGHT

By Diane Ackerman

THE PLANETS: A COSMIC PASTORAL

WIFE OF LIGHT

WIFE
OF
LIGHT

BY
DIANE ACKERMAN

WILLIAM MORROW AND COMPANY, INC.
NEW YORK   1978

Printed in the United States of America.

Library of Congress Cataloging in Publication Data

Ackerman, Diane.
    Wife of light.

    I. Title.
PS3551.C48W5   811'.5'4   77-25297
ISBN 0-688-03286-9

BOOK DESIGN AND BINDING   CARL WEISS

First Edition

1   2   3   4   5   6   7   8   9   10

ACKNOWLEDGMENTS

I am grateful to the editors of the following periodicals for first publishing some of these poems: *Aegis, Ambit, Carolina Quarterly, Chelsea, Chicago Review, Epoch, Granite, Iowa Review, Journal of General Education, Massachusetts Review, New Letters, Prairie Schooner, Remington Review, Slough,* and *Washout Review.* Some poems also appeared in the following anthologies: *The First Anthology, Intro 6 Anthology,* and *I, That Am Ever Stranger.*

Special thanks to A. R. Ammons and Paul West, who have read through the manuscript more times than anyone should have to.

CONTENTS

MOTHER

Mama's just blown in from Egypt,
full of mummy-lore, mishap,
river life, and beggars;
toting quietly-hued soapstone
scarabs, then fabric, jewels,
and bazaar-haggled goods;
pausing half a breath
to praise the guide
(savvy with hieroglyphics),
or damn the cuisine,
wince at the hygiene,
or, burbling spicy as the Nile,
hymn the *feluccas* at sunset,
whose huge linen sails,
bloating like ghosts,
patrol the slim swift river.

Round her neck she wears
a gold *cartouche* of her name:
hieroglyphs:
"cricket, bird, doorlatch, mouth, bird."
And yes, she *is* clicky and pert
as a cricket, twittery as a finch,
wedded to home-things
scrutably as a doorlatch,
gabby and bright, and game to fly off
to any grotto or seaport,
savanna or spa, glacier or oasis,
like a royal bird jaded by a single nest.

With her "Let's get crackin',"
and her "Howdja do,"
and her "Time's a-wastin',"
and her stiff coiffed hair,
and her soft winning smile,
and her livewire touring
from glowworm drippy caves
tilted deep in New Zealand
to Troy, Masada, Moscow or Bali Hai,

she is like a wild grain
waving its tassel
at the broiling summer sun:
an explosion of bud,
untroubled by pondering,
blues, or jet lag.
Churning and singable as the Nile,
she is life, and life
is what she brings.

NEW HOUSE

We bought a house hand-me-down
and complete, packed with all the gear
family life engenders: cameras,
clothing, junk and antiques,
vibrator, bowling ball, pans and glasses.

Every knick knack knows gossip
I have no right to, about a Mr. Norton
who lived, bred, and boozed there.
I'm told he died of gluttony
in middle age, towards the end

bloating like a pufferfish. Now
suddenly I've acquired
someone's life, as if it were a fondue pot
or a hedge cutter. His initial
still rules the hall linoleum.

There are mortgages and taxes
and a pool to skim daily,
poison ivy to uproot, grass to mow,
doors to lock. And me
with no steady job guaranteed.

Soon I'll leave the little garret
I've spent five years in, groomed
and combed and grown used to,
where I bedded my lover
and housed my jubilation, relaxed,

fretted, and pined, grew used to.
A roommate once had an afghan hound
with brown eyes like quicksand,
and such long spindly legs
it never could lie down right.

I used to watch
the poor beautiful creature
circle, fold and unfold and fold
its legs again, trying,
for all the world, just to settle.

ODE TO AN APPALOOSA STALLION

Spotted veteran of love,
you were made for fucking.
Wooing the mare with a tender nuzzle,
you rub her netherpetals
till they open
pink and sweet as a magnolia,
before you climb aboard
and set your hips a-bucking.

I see your white hide crawl,
black rosettes shudder
(like a scoopful of coal
dropping through snow),
and come alive
at the snort of your sunburnt nose,
your sweetbags twitching
peppery as stars.

If only I could have
the blunt fury of your limbs,
yowl and pump
like a desperado,
feel the sun on my neck
burning old as a motto,
then life coming,
the wheat spellbound in the fields.

SONG OF π

What lengths I've gone to
hoiking this gap-toothed
carcass up, as I barrel
out past horizon's bluff,
every digit pacing
like a Tennessee Walker,
unable to break even,
come round. Still,
I invent myself daily:
buxom 3's, coathanger 2's,
fetal 9's, 4's blowing
always to the west,
snowman 8's, runnel 1's,
and now and then
a single tantalizing 0
(whose frogspawn
could make one whole).
Thus I evolve, think,
quibble, and revise
on the spot, as though
daft with some perpetual
misgiving: 3.14 . . .
or rather 3.142 . . . I mean
3.1416 . . . no, 3.14159 . . .
ad infinitum . . . :
a concatenation of qualms

limping across the page
to no fixed result:
skittish, mazy,
decimated, unrepeating,
constant but runic,
at loose ends; while new
factors, a hair's breadth
more discrete, merely
winch the total sequence
tighter. Dwindling
ciphers trail behind me
like outmoded deities,
pleading to expire
in some perfect wholeness—
be finite, tally, nothing spare.
And so I hold out for that
wish-ribbed strand, perhaps
just over the next abscissa,
when the last of my last
fraction rounds off, and in one
spine-humming flash I feel
the common denominator
blaze through.

CRITICAL MASS

As I inch into Cayuga's neutral bed,
weeds begin to tick like fingers.

I can hear death hovering in the cell,
in the *cleat, cleat, cleat* of a wind-ripped

hickory, but am loath to unsaddle my mulish
brain of its radiant trappings: the fire -

bellied toads and mahogany horse chestnuts,
vegetarian crawdads digging down

to water level below the outlying cornfield,
the plaintive moan of an opossum's cantata.

And I am green to the tailwinds that gypsy
my thought so: gaping, misfit, and unplumbable.

Even the water spider seems to know
his belongings. I watch the plier legs open

and close, filled with the skittling lope
of him. And I am witless to the dynamo

revving my bustled heart when a siege of quail
fly cover at lake bend. And I am lame

to fathom this napalm wonder I cannot douse
even in the cool of the daybreak.

YOUR FUTURE MISTRESS

In your pockets my fingernails
red as satin ribbons
will alarm her, make her check
the closet and the door

Your backbone,
bruised and mapped: a river basin
and my eyes: brown worlds
orbiting in your throat

will conspire, make her vow
to drive me out of your limbs

Then you'll spend her like a coin
in your thighs' silk purse,
let her scrub me from your mind
like an old copper stain

And how shall I keep her
from that history
I cribbed
on your tongue's pliant web?

She'll say
Revenge is a dish which people of taste
prefer to eat cold   And set the teakettle
whimpering like a beaten dog

Then she'll claw me out of time, leave me
punctured, half-eaten, bleached dumb as bone

She'll prick a vein at your wrist
and unravel it to the heart, spread you
open like a fig
and cut my fever's root

16

CURTAINS OF GOLDENROD

Where curtains of goldenrod, dry
after their season's stiff yellow plume,
made hilltop a chamber, and a dozen blues
like confluent rivers of sky, met,
there, beneath the wild hay, you took me,
on a horseblanket, in a polar month,
sun hot on our heels, as well as our brains,
turning me nimbly on forehand and haunch,
while jets passed over like breaking waves.
I have scratches where the straw weeds chafed;
you made me willow like the bending grain.
Above, your eyes looked bluer than two ermine
in winter, bluer than the day's high nape.
Even the sky seemed to begin with your face.

HELEN-WHITNEY'S FLAT

Picasso's photo:
the bald man
cheeking his palm
like an advert
for denture cream.
A spray of Chinese
lanterns
stuffed with air
as monument to

17

the gluttony of nature.
The head of a cumbrous
vacuum cleaner,
scrubbed and polished
and arranged on top
of the filing cabinet.
With so many scallops
and convolutions
it looks like
a petrified insect
retching.
A horsehair couch
embalmed in plastic
flea collars.
A pair of clogs.
A black sling chair.
Two loafers patched
with mending tape.
An unchewed pencil
with no eraser
carefully curbing
a row of white pawns.
A castrated cat
skulking beneath
couch and table.
A dog-eared copy
of *le Surréalite*.
A crossword puzzle,
complete but for
the word "Bantu."
Paprika smuggled
from Budapest.
A vase of irises
gathered from
the adjoining yard.
An offprint.
A yawning figure.

WHERE PAUL WAS BORN

On a fog-cowled island
bobbing in the North Sea
like an iceberg —
little more than a chip
on Europe's shoulder;
next to the butcher shop
and across from the dry-goods
in a one-horse, twenty-pub,
cod-ridden town smackdab
in the Midlands, and called
Eckington;
hemmed in by coal mines
and the Sitwell acreage
where he first saw holly
growing wild: unplaited
and prickly all summer's
dead heat; in a row house
that sprawled up, not along
(flat iron warming
on the coals, chenille tablecloth
laid with empty jam jars
and mixed crockery, the gas light
begging for another penny);
three flights high
in an attic room overlooking
the Roman church and well spots
(from there to eye's limit,
khaki & green fields
sprouting wheat and cabbage);
in the blue bedroom,
under the eiderdown,
on a mattress fretted
with switchbacks and gullies;

out of a Saxon woman
with gray eyes, who was born
on Market Street,
married there, and, lifelong,
moved only ten yards or so;
through her tipped gullet:
queer, but sounder than my own;
knee-deep in her spine;
from a womb they unlatched
and tilted down like a chute;
covered with umbilical sackcloth
from the start, Paul landed
in this world on his feet.

GENETHLION

My Rex begonia has given birth.
When could it have happened?

At night, under the scallop
of the telephone wire
whose single hem stretches above western Pennsylvania?

Or in the open-throated morning
when sun poured down
the room like a thick yellow vitamin?

Look, how it dovetails to its mother.
Snug under one of her varicose palms,

it will make so little fuss
in this world, just praying for equilibrium,
biological Valhalla.

LAKEBED

Lying in your arms,
I watch, through the window,
the lake pump
 its blue blood to an icy froth.

Shorewise,
the waves knot hard, and roll
end over end
 clear down to the marina.

Gray cupolas fade
into the gray winter sky; already,
such a pyramidal mist
 is rising — over what? cloud? or mountain?

But I'm blind to form
in the abstruse sunlight. Roundabout
mid-lake,
 what I think a bass fisherman

I think is fishing;
all day, I see him lyrically bend and hoist,
bend and hoist,
 till light, crazing his boat,

dulls
to a thick blue shimmer.
By nightfall,
 when the whitecaps finally subside

(and yours, I notice,
have subsided, too), I grow, like the silent
liquefaction
 of your flesh, calmer and calmer.

QUIXOTE

What plagues the store-bought world is tedium.
Hash most nights. Beef shanks-and-sockets.
Lentils! On Sunday, boiled bones and *Te Deum*.
Buttoning and unbuttoning each other's pockets.

This night more sequined than a jaguar's hide
the moon is luminous, a white fleshy scar.
Time is a kneeling animal. People chide
me for being short of sense, but *they* are
short of wonder. Inbred. Inert. In cahoots. In lieu.
They spend their lives like dull brass coins,
while I crack open a world or two:
life's torpor is the blazing savanna of my loins.

So let me flail bug-eyed at a windmill's bark,
steal vision's pass key, rifle the dark.

NIGHTLETTER IN SEMAPHORE

A is not A it's B
say the neurons
chafing in the brain's
slippery locket.
And the snowy oaks
u-limbed like tuning forks
go into a rarely visible
octave of sky
where each branch runs
a brittle liaison
from the universe
to the dovegray planet below.

A is not A it's B
say the neurons
crackling in the brain's
echo chamber.
And the flat-black ceiling
of this winter night
suddenly waylays
a stand of poplars
by carving the negative
space all around them.
The air nearly curls
from one farm to the next.

A is not A it's B
say the neurons
sundancing in the brain's
gamy wet cell.
And tree-choirs become

mosques of intensity
whose black boughs
tolling above snow
set a knell
in my bones
like a Byzantine cathedral.

A is not A it's B
say the neurons
phrasing in the brain's
bloody minyan.
And in the sky
one jumbo jet
helps squander the night
on my focal plane
barnstorming
a yardarm deep into sense
until nothing remains
of my sanity but rumor.

A is not A it's B
say the neurons
yanking life inside out
like a sleeve, till grass
wails on its center
in bandit fury, or penguins refeed
a kind of marzipan soup.
A is never A
say the inputs
dropping through each cell
like pearls through a sizer, like dust
in a milkyway-station of flesh.

A is never never A
say the neurons
flying in the brain's
rapid transit:

a troupe of fools that signal
their lives in semaphore
to share a vision.
But one must speak so clearly.
And the neurons that never
never think more clearly
unhinge
every starry-throated night.

LIFE SENTENCE

Aside from the eggs like tiny appaloosas
cantering through my body's tide; the sun
always in the sky, and the ululation
of the seasons; aside from the winter/spring
polemic quibbling over a dry seedpod till it
sounds like a hooded mamba or a harpist;
aside from how grackles in a pile of hay
swear blue-jesus to con the moon into
one more spin around the dancing floor
and never notice the lean shafts lifting,
how *they* are lifting, till ploughed land's
widewale nap is lost in a flight of breakneck
clouds; aside from that vague psoriasis
of the spirit that threatens my bone-house
with foreclosure, the brainpantry teeming,
and the will as bloodthirsty as a tick; I mean
aside from all these obvious concessions,
I keep asking myself: what does gravity demand?

MENSTRUATION RAG

Played if you please
by tamponi and tuba
and accompanied by
an appropriate ritual,
say, snake, obsidian,
or the maw bone
of a buffalo, pouched
in deerskin and rattled
properly with a crisp *ye'ye'*.

But let's consider it
another way, as
theater in the round:
  "I've got dem low-down
  lunar cycle blues, daddy,"
the pitcher at the mound:
  "Two balls, one strike,
  and no outs, buster,"
one small drop for woman,
a hemorrhage for mankind.

For mankind no jam-rags,
powders, sprays, no mikvahs,
tampons, tablets, belts,
no breakthrough bleeding,
no calendar check meticulous
as a tornado watch,
no swearing on your life
in a busy cloakroom
that you're part
of the greatest show
on earth.

MYSTIC COMMUNION OF CLOCKS

There being no mystic communion of clocks
    it hardly matters when this autumn breeze
    wheeled down from the sun
    to make leaves skirt pavement like a million lemmings

An event is such a little piece of time-and-space
    you can mail it through the slotted eye of a cat
    we all pretty much agree
    words just fret the bowed neck of time

So it's nothing to say that at 96 below
    on this lovely fall day in arctic Siberia
    a young woman carried home her daily milk
    not in a bottle but under her arm in a slab

Or that precisely at five o'clock in the evening
    the Trans-Siberian Express tore streaks of iron
    from the vastness of nothing
    and ran hell-bent to the extremities of nowhere

MADAME BOVARY TO HER LOVER

Tuesday. The word sounds as far away
        as Florence. The backside of the moon
        is closer than tuesday!
   Tell me the winds, like a bagpipe skirling,
hail from a duchy
             fabulous as tuesday.
   The hot-blooded sun, now flitting
down my neck, now filling my room
     with its gold soliloquy,
   couldn't burn from a place
         more remote than tuesday.

My heart spends what it can least afford,
     a hundred times a day
           climbs aboard a jitney
   bound for tuesday; how shall I bear
its sweet treachery till tuesday?
         I'll work, I'll tidy, I'll garden,
  I'll do. I'll browse through scores
weighty as linen, but tuesday,
    tuesday dear as a pardon,

tuesday as unlikely as the Serengeti,
     tuesday, when you arch above me
   like a melody,
     when you sail through my limbs
on a breeze fresh as a colt,
   tuesday will harvest my mood,
my thought, tuesday rustle my whims,
     tuesday grow in my life
       like a weed.

A shadow, oblique, in a dream is tuesday!
    Only a China clipper, swayed off course,
      a tunic of kelp choking its bow,
might chance on an island
       extravagant as tuesday.
    Nut-sweet as tuesday. Lush and willowy
and green as tuesday. Come, swear to me
   that in your blithe pursuance
     of theater, *soirées,* and ortolans,
you won't know a savory breath
     till tuesday!

ST. AUGUSTINE CONTEMPLATING
THE BUST OF EINSTEIN

I

Selfless now in this crucible of light,
I act not by instinct, but rightly.
It's self-consciousness
that makes cowards of us all.
But the cloisters of my memory still
ring with visions of the concrete world,
that plane of one/many
riddling my life since *ex vacuo*.
Like you in my teens — a woolly
dream-gatherer — I worshiped the creature
over the Creator, prayed for
"chastity and continence, but not yet,"
then chained my senses together
like a great long molecule
blazing in some hyperbolic present.
I thought God dwelt in the motion of birds
rooting idly through damp sod,
or in their voluntary nervous system
of ducking their heads as they strut
in the cold. Skylocked, indigo branches
moved with more cadence than a Christian hymn.

II

But soon I became a house divided
between that geyser of color

and the asylum of God, *Fountain of Life*
and *Physician of my Soul.* Like you,
I blinkered my path to the essential,
ignored all the frippery that clutters up
the mind. You say photons clamor
eternally, and that speaks to me:
my first vision was one of infinite light.

III

But your principle of relativity
is as old as Galileo, who tried
to measure the speed of light
with two lanterns.
Your lanterns are planets,
and you conjure with such names
as One-Zwicky-One, Cygnus, and Orion,
prove your theorems with hydrofoils
that run on lubricated air.
I hear you've even computed
the circumference of the cosmos
(some exponential nightmare
reduced to ½ *a googol*),
but your gospel is no different
from Galileo's, only bolder:
you want to drive a stake
under the nail of the universe
and draw God out
like a soft-shelled crab.

IV

How elemental, the way you put it:
In the beginning
was the velocity of light.
But it means that God will never
be the same, now he's plummeted a peg
and had his secrets ogled.
You call this abomination Symmetry,
and that eludes me (light can behave
like a bullet or like the sound
of the shot, or like doubt
cruising silent as a white shark),
but when you say all is mutable,
that inflames me, because change
is contrary to the nature of God.
Where does that leave us?
Opting to face God or to face the Truth?
Or to face a God whose Truths are on tap,
some Holy Victim squatting on a pulsar?

Standing here bolt-still
(which is only to say: moving uniformly
at zero speed), I wonder if your myth
is right or just pretty, a kind of brainstem
sonata for μ-meson and cube root.
Tongue-tied, hamstrung, I feel battered
by answers that won't arrive for decades;
when they do, I suspect I'll find you
on the scaffold of the Knowable,
furiously soaping the noose.

GEORGE SAND, ADDRESSING
HER MIND, AT 50

Brain, old pensioner,
for years of loyal and fretful service,
what honorarium will do?
A silver watch
to tell minute vistas by,
while 60 cogs a minute
leave you, winded, to your slackening
haste?
A pen seeping bile
from its whale-black innards?

You, who never dressed before noon!
I find you out
early: doing sums, mending fences,
knitting yarns. Here,
let me clink my fork
against the glass,
rise to the occasion,
my shabby matron, my old grass-gypsy,

and swear, though you lie
in comic disarray,
      pilled, and pickled in your juices,
   your skirts frayed and gussetted,
      that you once ploughed furrows
straight as statutes,
        once, with your pack of hunting dogs,
   ran deep into far sloughy fields
to snare game,
     once hooted fashion,
     once tupped and raved,
once cheered, fueled, dabbled, quaffed,
tracked down, bled, bouqueted, and wallowed
        in ideas,
    covering their waterfront
     like a sailor's whore, who,
sleeping with all, belonged to none.

ANNE DONNE
TO HER HUSBAND

Come to bed, Jack, the candle's shed
to its waxy skirt, and I can read
    your straying wits by the moon.
A brain-fly must be buzzing your head!
    What is it now, that new ice, sheeting
the pond like a scald on hot milk? The swoon
    of dam-water, like a silent diphthong?
Lucky pond, to hold your gaze so long.

My eiderdown is greener than a glade;
you gave it me yourself, high
    when you dubbed me your *new found land,*
and swore, my continents your quest, you'd trade
    along the shores of my dark timbered eyes,
where unwooed lusheries of life meander,
    and time drops sail like a ketch in a lagoon.
Well, then, what keeps you?

Come away from the window!
You get ideas like other men catch cold.
    Mid-morning, a trifle waylaid you again,
and now your eyes, like twin hyenas,
    pick dinner in the slivery light
from the moon. Enough of your lyric flight!
    Enough peeking under the night's black shirt!
All day, you've been sickening with a verse.

For God's sake, quit gaming
with love, in poems abstruse, or as physical
        as if you were a physical
man. Maybe this one you'll title "Love's Dynasty,"
        and begin with a sunset, lying
on the horizon like an eel
        twitching its thick brown hide,
then hint at things matrimonial.

        And who'll guess that tonight, upright as an easel,
you've earth on the brain, not me.
        Though I'd tie you in lawless knots
if I could, my heart knows
        no rhetoric but your name,
Jack, that, like a doomed colonial,
        sails out with a seed-chest full of hope,
and raises so little crop.

        How can I compete with a vision?
What holy logic could my wiles defy?
        Your muse that's fat and sassy
as a cow, could I stint her even one
        of her piquancies? Her powwows? Her sprees?
What would it cost, in hard daily coin,
        if I shook you loose from this reverie?
I am not love's barrister (wish I were),

        but an offput woman on a night growing bleaker,
and night was never longer, or woman weaker.

SWEEP ME THROUGH
YOUR MANY-CHAMBERED HEART

Sweep me through your many-chambered heart
if you like, or leave me here, flushed
amid the sap-ooze and blossom: one more dish
in the banquet called April, or think me hard-
won all your days full of women. Weeks
later, still I felt your arms around
me like a shackle, heard all the sundown
wizardries the fired body speaks.
Tell me why, if it was no more than this,
the unmuddled tumble, the renegade kiss,
today, rapt in a still life and unaware,
my paintbrush dropped like an amber hawk;
thinking I'd heard your footfall on the stair,
I listened, heartwise, for the knock.

TRADESCANTIA FLUMINENSIS

My wandering plant spirals
out of its bowl, around the tabletop,
and down the walls,
crossing a bridge of itself
to the floor, where it sprawls
like a liver-green sylph.

Only *I* would pot a creeper,
but I wanted a plant more highly strung
than, say, an aster,
geranium, or even a breadfruit.
What rhododendron ever set the heart astir?
And a marigold is nothing to write home about.

I wanted a plant that would burgeon
from drink, badger the herb patch
till it died of famine,
seize the day lilies by the throat,
then flap around the seablue air like a salmon
and one day, god willing, keel over from gout.

A tentacled thing in the nature of a river.
A plant with backbone, no
jack-in-the-pulpit to sit up and beg.
Only this one does nothing but cantilever.
Its stems, trumpets, and whirligigs
each day and one by one grow fatter

mooching food in their stucco port.
I can hear each tiny siphon
finesse the liquid from the dirt,
chip minerals off the loam
like plaque, convert
the sun's bloodtide into phloem.

And, I'm afraid, I tend to collude
inasmuch as I sun, preen, and rotate
the pot, inasmuch as I flashflood
the etiolated roots with cocoon-like
passages of Strauss. Cowprod
by day and, by night, a sense-dike.

I'm wet nurse to a Machiavellian
potful of limbs
without ever knowing which one's
the spine that might
hang by its buds from the rafter one
morning, noose up my heels, and go for the throat.

I guess a backhand faith propels me.
That or a brand of Russian roulette.
I'll probably feed
the damn thing till I drop,
while it rigs tension-bridges and flees
over rivers that keep drying up.

A. R. AMMONS
AMID THE FUNGI

You say: segmented worms
roll back their saddles
during copulation.

And I say: yes, and pine bristles
like a boar's back.

And you say: red-capped fungi
will fabric the spring.

And I say: yes, and woodchucks
in hibernation are breathing
only ten times an hour.

And you say: shape & form & saliences.
And I say: verbal pliés, acoustic fatigue,

and do you read lodestars and cereal boxes?
And you say: yes, and navigation manuals,
place mats, and hurricane charts.

And I say: do you mind that it's colder
than a polar bear's menses? or that a cat
in a black hole in space becomes linguini?

I say: did you know that from Rimbaud
you get barium and radium, Bim, Bram,
mab, braid, drum, dram, daub, raid?

And you say: yes, and also bird & Brad,
Baird & Mau & Ra & Maud. And axolotl
is also good, have you tried vineyard yet?

And I say: yes, and that pockmarked
aluminum prop that we call a moon
answers directly to Mission Control.

And you say: yes, that trollop's
on a tether of Tang; she put the rill
in Rilke, you know what I mean?

And I say: yes, a bone knits and
a river purls, and I've always
admired your southern kraal.

And you say: jejune, and knee-deep
in the magma.
And I say: this is not the Hebrew letter
for Jehovah.

And you say: one thing about death —
it's hereditary.

And I say: where the hell are we
and, incidentally, how the hell is it here?
Isn't a friend someone to tread water with?

And you say: the asylum of idle chatter
is wide open.

ITHACA WITHOUT YOU

I'm sick of the night
deep as a lagoon,
its plum waters
crazed with larvae,
and the egret stars
picking, picking,
as their bills
garble moonlight
to fine glitter;

dog-tired of the spring days
thick as hops,
when seedpods lie wet
in their golden hulls,
and the streetlamps at dusk
echo and re-echo
a bluesy sun;

fed up with the *chee chee*
of the cardinals,
and the black quilted
cloud cover over the mountain,
and the hand-brogue
of the deaf-mute
across the road,
yes, and the loudmouthed
yahoo next door;

have had enough now
of the kites
circling, circling
like polishing rags,
and the lake tilting
its wet thighs
around a bend,
and the jet honing
a white arc
from zenith to horizon;

I'm sick to death
of all the Halloweens
and Easters,
and the neighbor girls
loping through the yard:
(each pelvis aflutter
like a pair of wings)
the mud ripe
in the mid-August heat,
the popsongs,
the gone-sours,
the setbacks, the blights,
the cartwheel heart
where love careens,
all the little dismals
and the giant dreams.

DRIVING THROUGH FARM
COUNTRY AT SUNSET

As I drive through farm country,
a damp reek brewing by the roadway
hits me. Manure, cut grass, honeysuckle,
spearmint. The air feels light as rusk.
And I want to lie down in the newly turned
earth, amid the wheat-chaff and the chicory,
while sunlight creeps up a mountainside

off in the distant whelm of color.
Each cemetery, flanked by poplars, looks ready
to play as a chess set. A dozen washloads
blow on the line, sock lanterns ablaze,
towels bellied like a schooner's rigging.
In a dogwood's petaled salon, bees leave
their pollen footprints as calling cards.

The occasional samba of a dragonfly
tightens the puffy-lidded dusk.
Clouds begin to curdle overhead. And I want
to lie down with you in this boggy dirt,
our legs rubbing like locusts'.
I want you here with the scallions
sweet in the night air, to lie down with you
heavy in my arms, and take root.

NOX

Sleep is philatelical: now and then
I hinge a raggedy night into the album
by focusing on the pier where
inhalation departs and exhalation returns
on a counterwhim, but my brain rarely
cottons to closing down. Giving up the day
is like giving up the ghost. Oh, I know
sleep is a graving dock for the cells
and, come morning, I'll glide down
a daylight slipway, spanking new, or
pervious at least and rehulled. It's not
sleep that ushers in the earthworm's banquet,
not thought that commits me to the future,
but at night, face down in the pyramidal
blackness, when a 30-caliber callus
ought to be deadening my brain, I see
cosmic simooms of flocculent white gas;
the backbone's chain of tiny voodoo skulls;
the mob-law of the asteroids.

DIGGING HOLES

I dug an icy shovel
through the grass,
leaning my weight
until the earth buckled.
Loam clung to the spade
like mocha fudge,
as I scooped out
a tidy pit.

A half-dug hole
seems an open cause,
knows where it's going,
has depths,
even if wrongplaced.
And so I delved,
reamed and gouged,
until the hole
nearly swallowed me up,
and people flocked round
to ooh and ah
at the depth.

It was a good hole,
             solid, flannel-banked.
But I rarely saw
      the candle-pine or hickory,
                      and to be sure
            no leaves
      waddling across the road
                  like a herd of penguins.
            Only the moon
      white as a sand dollar.

                        So I climbed out
and moved a few yards
        beyond the beech tree,
      where hibiscus
                  rolled its saucy tongue,
drove my blade
            into older soil,
            and began again.

PERIOD PIECE

Moon, whose name I bear, whose likeness
like a coin I wear on my thigh,

Moon bleeding light across the sky,
tally me a bonus month on your ledger,

before this light and tender anger swells.
You who fan the fever in my cells,

who take a fine fettle and curdle it brainsick,
or turn a heart bright as nettle rash

choleric, Moon be ghostly, run your rings
round me with sweet dereliction,

drain the red lava from my womb
if you must. Grip my bowels with cramps

thick as a simoom, but spare me
the trumpeting frets and the jealousies,

the love-yowls, the warps of reason,
the willies, the riptides, the alarms,

the old woes I exhume like unquiet corpses,
the boo hoos, and the dread,

the nuggets of self-pity glowing
like ore in a swamp-black season.

Moon, white as garlic
in the cauldron of my misery,

today your silent weather in the vein
swept through my bone-house

like a cyclone, cut the delicate seines
my trawlers fix in wonder's lush terrain,

bowled a shock wave so razing
my bubbly spirits decanted to still-wine.

Cares that daily fade or lie low
hogged front-row-center in the bleachers

of my despair and there, solemn
as kewpie dolls, began to heckle and hoot.

My lover I tried to box into absolutes,
pelting him with a cairn of chaos.

I hung round his neck like an albatross.
I told him my heart was black as a nimbus,

squirrely, young, and disloyal as dross,
then watched his eyes grow heavy as ingots.

Moon, I am like a carpet you flog.
I, who am too far from the cave

for worship, too far from the grave
to nod and cry quits, where do I send my protest,

my plea? Whom do I lobby for redress,
what throat do I slit on what altar?

Moon, in whose lumbering wake
my blood swarms, humor me: stand still

in the heavens, deliver me from all this
dolor and fugue (I'd sooner

you looted my soul than my mood),
spare me your rod and your cane.

Pale goblin I waltz with each night,
if you fancy me so, feed your ivory yen

and drink my fluids all, espouse me,
wed me to oblivion. For I am like a heron

on your South China junk. Slip off
the gold wafery collar that keeps

mortality but a swallow away,
and you can clasp me forever

to your wide white chest,
make me your concubine, your dalliance.

Snatch me now in the dead of night.
Only, Moon, be merciful to your wife of light.

I SHOULD HAVE TREKKED
WITH SCOTT TO ANTARCTICA

I should have trekked with Scott to Antarctica
and ditched my ghost there, so I'd be numb
as prairie ice by now, free from love's arsenic
to-ing and fro-ing, my hope fitful as a swannery.

I should have lived heartsimple as a nun,
worn my habits like silk, said buckshot *Hail Mary*s,
been exempt from the fiery greens of summer
and your gaze overflowing my saucer eyes.

I should have been a thermal, or the windage
in a breeze left by the swift absence of a nighthawk,
been immune to all the heady fret and vigil
when doubt sails cockeyed as an ice yacht.

Or I should have been a gypsy fit to besot you,
rivet you with spells, puzzle and haunt you,
ripe as a pomegranate, a sensual stampede,
not this plain young woman with an abstract need.

TRELAWNY PARISH, JAMAICA

Scanning the beach:
a sail distends its bubble throat
like a lizard in heat, stray cats
go slow-gait through palms and mimosas
toying with the carcass of a beetle,
sandfleas tick away at my heels
like Kamikaze pilots.

                In the kitchen
Millicent scales red snapper; the silk fish
we'll eat on the veranda.

I can account for hydra-headed coral,
atomic weights, salmonella poison,
beetles surviving unchanged for centuries,
lemur feet flat as tiny pancakes,
even life in a pocket of RNA.

But as for how all flesh arose
from that slimy web of muck and weed,
how eyes, brains, nerves sprang
from the interface of plankton and mammal,

all I hear is the thunder of water
on a tin sieve. Crash and caterwaul
as waves crack bone off the coral reef:
an orchestrated bribe, perhaps,
nothing less than lunacy.

MOONING

"When I approach, you stiffen
like an egg white. Can't get a rise
      out of you at all," I said.

Gargoyle moon just stared.

"But even the bat, blinded
      and with half a voice,
spends his life trying
      to kick against the bricks."

Moon shrugged an icy shoulder.

I said, "I know the sun,
      hemorrhaging light,
grabs back a smidge: reluctant,
not wanting to give all.
      But you can't turn
another cheek forever."

The badgered moon spun round
on its heel and snapped,
      "What *do* you want?"

"Oh moon," I said, "uncan me
like a brisling sardine, fluke me out
      past ad infinitum galaxies
barnacle-clinging to the cosmic bow.

"I want to tour far-flung stellar
quarries, and hightail it back again
          when the spirit moves me.
Reinvest this dark rubbery form
a quorum of my atoms upkeep."

The moon said, "What a mouthful.
          Wise up and forget it."

I said, "Listen, you bull-headed
          white cyst, you salty old mote
on the night's backside. . . ."

Moon flexed his magnetic taws
like a nautilus and said, "Watch it.
          You're out of your league."

I said, "Moon, honey,
you've got me by the short hairs.
          Step down for a day or two
and I'll lather your rills,
          make your lava run,
I'll take your breath away."

The moon blushed tawny rose
and said, "Any time.
          You just sashay on up."

THE BATHROOM CURTAIN
HAS A WAY OF DROOPING

The bathroom curtain has a way of drooping
till the woods out back lie hidden.
So always, in tub or on porcelain throne,
I pull aside the window shawling, slowly,
like a courtesan's robe, to fix on the lusty
undergrowth or tree limbs nodding like stags:
all things brute, zesty, time-culled.

These days, I can't pull the curtain aside
without thinking how, in bed, you
draw my tumbly hair out of lips and eyes,
perhaps to see your handiwork mull
my face like cider while the world's retreating.
Or do my reptilian pupils lure you,
their black fuses lit and bloodwings beating?

ENTREATY

Sir, if you love me, hold me to life
              as to a promise,
provide for my ramshackle age.
Never will I be gibbous like the moon,
childfull and eager
              all the tot-centered day.
Though I conjure pelicans
              out of ice-tinged barbwire,
or lathe heaven into a shrinkproof hour,
others know by instinct
              what I never learned:
how to crochet raggedy minutes into spells,
              spells into days.

Sir, if you love me, teach me to collect
              my galloping hopes;
how to jam work's merciful fabric

into each hollow of a routine month;
how to greet life
              blazing like the pillars of Troy
and not char to rubble, not turn sour;
how to trot out and lunge the stabled heart
on riderless calms
              in the deathwatch of winter.

Sir, if you love me, teach me to thrive
without you,
              to be my own genesis.

THE ELEMENTS

Her face. She forms it
with the pepper of makeup
on skin gelled clean,
daubs on philters
that haven't changed
since Grecian girls
picked wild tansy
to warm their cheeks
like seaslopes bending
the Mediterranean sun.

She pore-tugs
with astringent ice,
beauty grains, and the pulpy
green meat of an avocado.
Scoured, her face feels
brittle as taffeta, and
ready for its slipstream
of super-luminous gloss.
Color she doles out
like black-currant jam.

What she tells herself
varies from day to day: she's
a victim of habit, washed-out,
or wan, or an *echt* modern woman,
or a Creole artist. And besides,
who can say it's not Quechua
warpaint — tom-tom of rouge
drummed into the bone? Anything
but that grave in the cell.

Each morning she rebegins
her saga of color: bugle-shaped
eyes drawn black as lava
float gaily on phosphorescent lids.
She dips into her bag of notions
for some salve to make her toll
like a bell rung by Abelard,
or cast by El Greco:
Scheherazade of the bathroom,
victim of the molecule.

ATLANTIC MOONFISH

Nacreous, thin,
12 inches long,
with an enormous
cranium
and tinselly scales,
it puckers its lips
voluptuously.
I remember
Nabokov said
nymphets
do not occur
in polar regions.
This one
sidles up
to the glass,
bald-faced,
like a white
corpuscle
on the playground
of Dr. Caligari,
swell-bellied
and thoroughly
afflicted
with itself.
It winks one
transparent eyelid,
glowers
and struts
like a bandit
then, cocksure,
drains off
the last
of my
existence.

OF COURSE
THE EARTH WON'T STOP

Of course the Earth won't stop
if you never uprush my steps again,
all winning talk and agile limbs.
The whiskery mountains,
in whose 5 o'clock shadow we loved, won't up
and fly apart. Geese will mob again,
blackening the sky like a shake of pepper,
coffee beans still look like tiny twats, paupers
sign their names with a flourish,
cattle moan like banshees to be fed, the Earth
go on its green, evitable way,
full of come-hither meadowgrass
waving and waving
and waving, under a moon round as an abbess.

Only life's eager whittler will hollow
me out by seconds, chip bark
off living wood, my heart
lie thwarted as a wing-clipped swallow
each time I confuse its muffled beating
for your heel-skip on the landing.
I'll remember how we loved: hot
and smoking as the Caribbean sun,
and the blues will settle in my ribcart
like a fog, my spirit blight, my shanties rot.
Days
will drag their long carcasses on
forever, dull as ditchwater, blank arrays.
Then loss will jimmy my bones apart,
till I die from the draft in my heart.

ADDENDUM

And isn't it enough that the mind's caliper
widens to take in a log, can also

accommodate the hollow bones of a blackbird
flying elliptically to pinion a field,

does not overlook the sun bleaching the sky,
or how pinecone trees effloresce

into a highrise of spiny sea urchins and then
handgrenades frozen at the moment of explosion,

and never misses the dark hot muscle of a tuna;

I've got lots of sensibility and no common sense;
isn't it better to lie low while the universe bombards,

to ride out the pendulation of the seasons,
straining not so often to embrace the moon, but more

to render it embraceable; isn't it enough
that one branch, rocking before a storm, can gather

the lines of twilight like threads in cool fresh sheets;
and isn't it enough that all creeks flow seaward;

isn't it enough that riverbanks come in pairs?

ODE TO THE ALIEN

Beast, I've known you
in all love's countries, in a baby's face
knotted like walnut meat,
in the crippled obbligato
of a polio-stricken friend,
in my father's eyes
pouchy as two marsupials,
in the grizzly radiance
of a winter sunset, in my lover's arm
veined like the blue-ridge mountains.
To me, you are beautiful
until proven ugly.

Anyway, I'm no cosmic royalty
either: I'm a bastard of matter
descended from countless rapes
and invasions
of cell upon cell upon cell.
I crawled out of slime;
I swung through the jungles
of Madagascar;
I drew wildebeest on the caves at Lascaux;
I lived a grim life
hunting peccary and maize
in some godforsaken mudhole in the veldt.

I may squeal
from the pointy terror of a wasp,
or shun the breezy rhetoric
of a fire;
but, whatever your form, gait, or healing,
you are no beast to me,
I who am less than a heart-flutter
from the brute,
I who have been beastly so long.
Like me, you are that pool
of quicksilver in the mist,
fluid, shimmery, fleeing, called life.

And life, full of pratfall and poise,
life where a bit of frost
one morning can turn barbed wire
into a string of stars,
life aromatic with red-hot pizzazz
drumming ha-cha-cha
through every blurt, nub, sag,
pang, twitch, war, bloom of it,
life as unlikely as a pelican, or a thunderclap,
life's our tour of duty
on our far-flung planets,
our cage, our dole, our reverie.

Have you arts?
Do waves dash over your brain
like tide rip along a rocky coast?
Does your moon slide
into the night's back pocket,
just full when it begins to wane,
so that all joy seems interim?
Are you flummoxed by that millpond,
deep within the atom, rippling out to every star?
Even if your blood is quarried,
I pray you well,
and hope my prayer your tonic.

I sit at my desk now
like a tiny proprietor,
a cottage industry in every cell.
Diversity is my middle name.
My blood runs laps;
I doubt yours does,
but we share an abstract fever
called thought,
a common swelter of a sun.
So, Beast, pause a moment,
you are welcome here.
I am life, and life loves life.